THE COMPLETE BOOK OF THE NIGHT

Sally Tagholm

KINGFISHER

Editor   Hannah Wilson
Designer   Jane Buckley
Production   Caroline Hansell
DTP manager   Nicky Studdart
Picture research manager   Jane Lambert
Picture research   Juliet Duff and Audrey Reynolds

The publisher would like to thank the following illustrators:
Andrea Brun (Luigi Galante), Julian Baker, Julian Baum, Peter Dennis
(Linda Rogers Associates), Ceri Llewellyn, Ray Grinaway, Keith Hume, Josephine Martin,
David Rushby, Roger Stewart (Kevin Jones Associates) and Gareth Williams

The publisher would also like to thank the following people:
Valerie Barclay, Julie Ferris, Jennie Morris, Dr Phill Read, Jane Tassie and Ben Wilson

The publisher would also like to thank the following for supplying photographs:
Mountain Camera Picture Library/John Cleare: 8cl; The Bridgeman Art Library/The Victoria
& Albert Museum: 9tl; Science Photo Library/NASA: 9cr; Art Directors & Trip Photographic
Library/H Rogers: 12tl; Science Photo Library/James Holmes/Janssen Pharmaceutical Ltd: 13br;
The Stock Market/Pete Saloutos: 23br; gettyone/Stone/Glen Allison: 24bl; Science Photo Library/
Klaus Guldbrandsen: 25tl; The Art Archive: 27tr; Corbis: 31cr, 37tr; gettyone/Stone/Mike
McQueen: 40tl; Robert Harding Picture Library/L Taylor: 41tr; Collections/Brian Shuel: 41cr;
NHPA/Eric Soder: 44tl; Science Photo Library/George Post: 44bl; Bruce Coleman Collection/
KimTaylor: 49cr, br; gettyone/Stone/Chad Slattery: 64cl; The Aviation Picture Library: 65cr;
Science Photo Library: 71br, 90br, 91tr; Corbis: 82–83; NASA: 88tl, cl, bl, 89tr, cr, br
Every effort has been made to trace the copyright holders of the photographs.
The publisher apologizes for any inconvenience caused.

KINGFISHER

Kingfisher Publications Plc
New Penderel House, 283–288 High Holborn
London WC1V 7HZ
www.kingfisherpub.com

First published by Kingfisher Publications Plc in 2001
2 4 6 8 10 9 7 5 3 1

1TR/0501/TWP/CLSN/150SMA

ISBN 0 7534 0528 8

Printed in Singapore

CONTENTS

NIGHT FALLS

As the Sun sinks below the horizon,
draining the Earth of its warmth
and light, the Moon waits quietly
in the sky, ready to cast its pale glow
into the darkness. For many, it is
the end of a day, a time to sleep,
but for others, it is just the beginning…

BEDTIME

As darkness falls, it's time to brush your teeth and get ready for bed. Bedtime always seems to come too soon, but there is nothing like being tucked up in your own bed, drifting off to sleep. But what happens when we sleep? Where and why do we sleep? What are dreams? Bedtime is an adventure we have every night without really knowing much about it.

Beds

Beds come in all sorts of shapes and sizes – from tiny cots for babies to king-size, four-poster beds for those who like a little luxury. If you're out and about, you need to carry a light, practical bed that fits in with your adventures.

Whatever type of bed you have, make sure it's comfortable – your body needs a good rest every night. Firm beds are the best as they give your back good support while you sleep. Don't forget that beds can be fun, too – there are bunk beds, water beds, sofa beds and even beds shaped like cars or spaceships! King Louis XIV of France loved staying in bed so much that he often held court there. He had a collection of 413 different beds!

Mountaineers often spend the night halfway up snowy mountains. Their beds are portable ledges, or portaledges, which they secure to the rock face. The ledges are just big enough to sleep on, tucked up inside a sleeping bag. The climbers sleep wearing harnesses attached separately to the rock, so that if the ledges fall from the mountain in the night, the climbers won't!

In the past, mattresses were stuffed with straw or feathers and did not have any springs. The bases of beds were often criss-crossed ropes, which were tightened regularly to stop them sagging – this explains the expression 'sleep tight'. In cool climates, people once slept under thick blankets and wore nightcaps to keep warm. Today, central heating, electric blankets and snug duvets keep out the cold at night.

The Great Bed of Ware is a huge, elaborately carved, four-poster bed, built at the end of the 16th century in England. It first stood in the town of Ware in an inn, possibly as a tourist attraction because of its enormous size. The story goes that it was once so big that it could sleep as many as 68 people!

Ancient Egyptians slept on narrow, wooden beds, and instead of pillows, they used small neck rests. In Japan today, many people sleep on futons – mattresses that are stored in cupboards in the day and rolled out onto tatami mats at night. Jungle explorers like hammocks as they can be hung between trees above muddy ground and away from curious animals. Mosquito nets, soaked in inspect repellent, ward off unwelcome night-flying bugs.

There is no gravity in space so astronauts sleep in tethered sleeping bags that don't float away. These beds can point in any direction – even upright – as there is no up or down in space. Sleep is timetabled – there is no day or night in space either. Sometimes mission control back on the Earth plays music to wake the astronauts!

9

Toothy tales

Roman emperors used to have special slaves to clean their teeth for them, but you probably don't – so remember to brush your teeth before you go to bed!

Germs can build up around your teeth and gums in the night, causing tooth decay and bad breath. To avoid this, brush the outside, inside and biting surfaces of your teeth for about two minutes in the morning and at night.

In the past, people used small sticks to clean their teeth. Today, we use hi-tech toothbrushes – even electric ones. We also use modern toothpastes that contain fluoride. Long ago, strange pastes and powders were used. They contained all sorts of ingredients – even egg shells and dried flowers! No wonder it's always been a good idea to spit toothpaste out!

10

When one of your first 'milk' teeth drops out, don't forget to hide it under your pillow before you go to bed. Some people think that the Tooth Fairy may pay you a visit in the night to collect it. If you are very lucky, she will leave a few shiny coins in return.

The Ancient Egyptians treated toothache by pressing warm, dead mice against their cheeks over the painful spot – a treatment not recommended today! If you do have toothache, see your dentist, and try to cut down on sugary snacks and drinks, which can cause the problem.

When it is really hot, crocodiles wallow in the water and open their mouths wide to cool themselves down. Sometimes birds perch inside their mouths and hop about, pecking out insects and bits of food that are stuck in their teeth – just like living toothpicks!

Sleeping

Most of us spend about a third of our lives asleep, recharging our batteries ready for the next day. Sleep is so important that we can survive longer without food than we can without sleep. It's no wonder Napoleon I, the French general and emperor, failed when he tried not to sleep at all!

When we sleep, our pulse rate and blood pressure drop and our breathing slows. This gives our body and brain a chance to rest. Growth hormones are released in children when they sleep, so sleep helps them to grow. Sleep also helps the proteins in our cells that keep us looking healthy. Sleep really is 'beauty sleep'!

When some people are anxious or over-tired, they walk or talk in their sleep. Others grind their teeth, and many people are loud snorers. But as we often experience amnesia, or forgetfulness, after sleep, it is difficult to know exactly what happens when we sleep.

Different animals need different amounts of sleep – the giant armadillo, one of the laziest animals around, needs about 18 hours at a time, but giraffes sleep for only two hours. The brains of bottle-nosed dolphins are divided into halves that take it in turn to sleep. This means that the dolphins can swim about and sleep at the same time.

Five tips that might help you to get a good night's sleep

1. Try to go to bed and wake up at the same times to get your body used to a routine.
2. Avoid tea and fizzy pop as they often contain caffeine, which may keep you awake.
3. If you can, try to do a little exercise every day, but not just before bedtime.
4. Have a bath before you go to bed – the heat will help your body to relax.
5. If you can't sleep, don't lie awake worrying about it. Try reading a book in bed.

Your age affects how much sleep you need. Babies need about 16 hours sleep, adults about eight hours, and elderly people often need as little as four hours. You probably need about ten hours sleep – the same as a dog!

The Native American Ojibwas, or Chippewas, weave magical webs to hang from babies' cradles. These 'dream catchers' are made from willow hoops, plant fibres and feathers, which symbolize breath or air. It is believed that the webs catch all the bad dreams, but allow good dreams to slip through to the babies.

Dreaming

People have always been fascinated by the strange and shadowy world of dreams, and have tried to make sense of it in all sorts of different ways.

In the ancient world, dreams were believed to be messages from the gods – either warnings or predictions – and were taken very seriously. Special dream interpreters, often priests or priestesses, were used to decode these divine communications and to unravel all their mysteries.

Today, scientists believe that sleep is divided into 'dreaming' and 'non-dreaming'. Each night, when you drift off to sleep, your brain ticks over on autopilot, chewing things over. After about 90 minutes, you emerge from deep sleep and enter dreaming sleep. This is when you have those hair-raising adventures, strange encounters and odd experiences, like running furiously but getting nowhere, flying high in the sky or falling down a dark, bottomless pit.

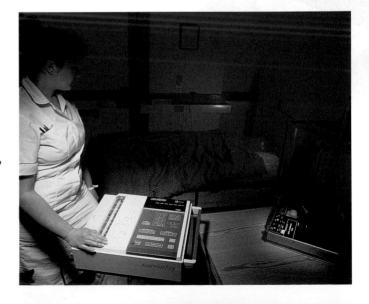

Scientists in special sleep laboratories conduct research into patterns of sleep and dreaming. They glue small electrodes to the scalps of volunteers to detect brain activity, and to areas around the eyes to monitor eye movement. The information is recorded and analyzed.

Today, some people still believe that dreams have important meanings. By analyzing the content of your dreams, they feel that they can reveal something about an aspect of your life or even predict something about your future.

If you dream of pirates, you will have an adventure.

A dream about ice cream means you will be successful.

Dream of an ear and you will hear startling news.

Dreaming of strawberries brings happiness.

An umbrella is a symbol of security.

Dreaming of birds is lucky.

During dream sleep, the body is paralyzed by the brain and will not move at all except for rapid eye movements and twitches of hands or feet. This paralysis protects the body from injury by allowing the sleeper to dream about adventurous activities without actually going as far as performing them in bed!

Dreaming sleep is also known as Rapid Eye Movement (REM) sleep because, when you dream, your eyes move about beneath your eyelids. REM lasts for about 20 minutes and occurs at least five times every night, causing vivid dreams – even if you don't remember them all!

Pyjama party

If you are very lucky and very nice to
your parents, every once in a while, you may
be allowed to stay up past your bedtime
for a pyjama party or a midnight feast!

Sneak down to the kitchen
for some night-time nibbles.
A midnight menu should be
simple – avoid rich foods, such
as cheese and chocolate, which
are hard to digest late at night.

Pyjamas, originally
from India, were
first worn around the
house during the day.
The word 'pyjamas'
comes from the
ancient Persian and
Urdu for 'leg' ('pae')
and 'clothing' ('jamah').

Plan your sleepover party carefully.
It's best to have it at the weekend
or during the holidays, so that you don't
have to wake up very early the next day.
Don't invite too many people – it's lots
more fun with just your closest friends.

No pyjama party is complete without games. To play Chinese Whispers, everyone sits in a circle, and one person thinks up a sentence – it could be funny, tongue-twisting or spooky. The sentence is whispered from person to person around the circle. The last person to hear the message has to say it out loud. How much has the message changed from its original version?

To play Wink Murder, get a few slips of paper – the same number as there are players. Write 'M' for 'murderer' on one, 'D' for 'detective' on another and leave the rest blank. Fold up the bits of paper and let everyone choose one, reading the slips in secret. Then, everyone sits in a circle and silently looks at each other. The murderer can 'murder' people by winking at them. If you are winked at, fake a dramatic death and remain 'dead' for the rest of the game. The murderer must try to murder everyone without being caught by the detective, who must spot the murderer mid-wink and reveal his or her identity to win the game.

Ghost stories can be good fun. Turn out the lights and tell some spooky tales. But remember, they are only stories – nothing to be afraid of!

Shine a torch or bedside lamp against a wall and try to make these hand shadows. Can you invent any others?

Standing between the light and the wall, bend your arm into the shape of a swan's neck. Make the head and beak with your hand.

Cross your hands over each other and link your thumbs. Can you see a bird, butterfly or night-time bat? Try to make it flap its wings.

Make a dog shadow by bending your index finger and sticking your thumb up. Then, lower your little finger to open the dog's mouth.

An A to Z of night fun

We associate all kinds of things with night – stars, ghosts and UFOs. When you sort the facts from the fiction, the night can be great fun!

Astronomy is the study of our night sky and the whole of the Universe.

Baba Yaga, a fictional Russian witch, flies through the air in a kettle!

Candles made from beeswax or animal fat lit homes at night long ago.

Darkness is nothing to fear – it just makes things a bit harder to see!

Equinox, 'equal night', occurs when night and day are the same length.

Frogs often croak loud, night-time choruses to try to attract mates.

Ghosts are spooky spirits that some people think come out at night.

Hekate is the Ancient Greek goddess of ghosts, magic and witches.

Imps are tiny fantasy figures that may play naughty, night-time tricks!

Jack-o'lanterns are Hallowe'en lamps made of hollowed-out pumpkins.

Kakapos are night parrots from New Zealand that look like owls.

Lantern festivals light the darkness in many parts the world.

Moonrats are tiny, hairy Asian mammals that creep out at night.

Nightmares were once thought to be monsters sitting on people's chests.

Owl monkeys, or night monkeys, have large, round, yellow eyes.

Poltergeists are spirits that some people blame for night-time noises.

Quivering and quaking? But there's no need to be afraid of the night!

Radishes are sculpted and celebrated on a special night in Mexico!

Stars twinkle and sparkle in the vast darkness of our night skies.

Twilight is the soft light that falls between sunset and darkness.

UFOs, unidentified flying objects, are sometimes seen at night.

Vampires are fantasy creatures that drink blood and hate daylight.

Werewolves are fictional people who turn into wolves at full Moon.

X,Y,Z are x-files, yetis and...zzz, zzz...time for bed!

NIGHT
LIGHTS

Long ago, before electricity and light bulbs
arrived, nights could be as black as ink.
Lighting the darkness has always been
a matter of necessity, but also of pleasure –
think about the importance of a lighthouse,
guiding ships into port, or the beauty of
a firework display, illuminating the skies
in every direction for kilometres around.

The lighthouse

For thousands of years, light has been used as a signal. From the top of lighthouses, fires burned brightly to ships at sea, and bonfire beacons blazed from hilltops to warn of invasion. Today, electric lamps send out very powerful beams of light.

Lighthouses flash their huge lights into the night seas to guide ships towards harbour or away from rocks. Most boats and ships have on-board navigation systems, but sailors still rely on the comforting glow from a lighthouse – especially if their systems fail! The beam from a lighthouse is reflected through lenses and shone directly at the horizon – no light is wasted by being sent towards the sky or the sea. The strength of the beam is measured in 'candelas'. A beam of 100,000 candelas can be seen about 40 kilometres away.

The first-known lighthouse was built more than 2,000 years ago on the island of Pharos in the ancient port of Alexandria, Egypt. At more than 100 metres high, it was the Earth's tallest structure at the time. From its top, a huge fire blazed, turning the night sky a deep red. It is thought that a metal mirror reflected the light from the fire up to 50 kilometres. The lighthouse had three main sections – a box-shaped column, an octagonal pillar and a cylinder on top. Clad in dazzling white marble, this amazing structure is one of the Seven Wonders of the Ancient World.

Lighthouses are beacons – light signals used to communicate messages. In the past, beacons were usually small fires. Chains of beacons were used as early-warning systems. The beacons were lit, one by one, on hilltops, towers and walls to pass news over long distances – sometimes hundreds of kilometres. In 1588, the Spanish Armada – a fleet of 130 ships – was spotted approaching England, and a chain of bonfires was lit along the English coast to warn of the attack.

Perhaps the most famous beacon is the Olympic flame. Every four years, a torch is lit from the Sun's rays in the ancient stadium in Olympia, Greece, where the Olympic Games began more than three thousand years ago. Over several months, thousands of runners relay the torch through many countries to the opening ceremony of the Games. For the 2000 Olympics in Sydney, Australia, the flame briefly travelled underwater, carried as a burning flare by a scuba diver.

Night shine

To get by in our night-time world, we rely on many different forms of light – from tiny cat's-eyes that wink light along dark roads to huge neon signs that shine their messages to whole cities.

Luminous things glow in the dark. Some reflect light given off by other objects – road signs shine when they reflect the light from car headlights. Shiny, smooth, bright materials, such as mirrors, make the best reflectors.

Light bulbs produce their own light when electric currents are passed through wires inside the bulbs. Electricity can also cause gases such as neon to glow orange and red.

Ultraviolet is a form of radiation. It makes some materials glow in the dark. People can label their possessions with special ink, visible only under ultraviolet light, so if they are stolen and then recovered, they can be identified.

The electric lights of Las Vegas dominate the night skyline of the Nevada desert, USA. The city buzzes and glows with activity non-stop – you can shop, visit a casino and even get married in the middle of the night! Along a road known as 'The Strip', 25,000 kilometres of neon tubes and thousands of light bulbs create amazing displays – there is a huge exploding volcano and a replica of France's Eiffel Tower!

Luminous watches glow in the dark so that we can tell the time during the night. The hands and numbers on their faces are coated with a special chemical that produces light. Televisions and computer monitors also glow in the dark. Their screens are made up of tiny dots that glow red, green or blue when electrons are fired at them. From a distance, moving colour pictures are seen.

Cat's-eyes lie at intervals along the middle of roads and reflect the headlights of cars at night, so that drivers can follow the bends in the road ahead. The 'eyes' are reinforced glass, shaped to reflect as much light as brightly as possible. The glass is protected in rubber cups and sunk into the road.

25

Fireworks

From a tiny sparkler twinkling in the night to a huge rocket exploding into a thousand shining stars, fireworks are used all over the world in celebration. They have beautiful, exotic or even alarming names – Silver Rain, Jewelled Pyramid or Mine of Serpents.

Fireworks were probably invented in ancient China, where gunpowder was discovered 2,000 years ago. One ingredient of gunpowder is saltpetre, which is found throughout China and Asia. Saltpetre, or 'Chinese snow', is still used to make fireworks. It is mixed with charcoal and sulphur and packed into hollow, paper tubes to create the most traditional of all fireworks – rockets.

A rocket is launched when the fuse attached to the gunpowder mixture inside is set alight. The jet of fire and gases produced propels the rocket into the sky. Once the rocket is in the air, further explosions cause a spectacular firework display.

Fireworks probably spread to Europe in the 13th century, but it wasn't until the 19th century, when new chemicals were added to the original gunpowder recipe, that a variety of sparkles and stars, bangs and hisses became possible.
It was discovered that different chemicals produced different colours – chemical compounds of sodium produce yellow and compounds of strontium produce red. Compounds of copper, mixed with chlorine gas, produce blue.

Firecrackers, which produce loud bangs and only tiny sparks, are the earliest form of modern fireworks. They were first used in ancient China to honour the gods and to celebrate weddings, births, battle victories and eclipses of the Moon. Today, 'crackers' are still used in China for the most important traditional use – frightening evil spirits away from homes.

Firework displays are also called 'pyrotechnics', which means 'skill with fire' in Ancient Greek.

Early fireworks were adapted from military rockets and missiles, and some forms of fireworks are still used today in warfare – 'star shells' are used to light up battlefields and 'parachute flares' illuminate landing areas for aircraft. Other flares and rockets are used as warning or distress signals, and many sailors and mountaineers carry them in case of emergency.

WARNING: All fireworks are dangerous. They can and do cause serious injury. They must be set off by adults only. In many countries, fireworks are illegal and can only be handled by experts during organized pyrotechnic displays.

Special Nights

Throughout the ages, people from all over the world have had different ideas about the night. While some have feared it, most have enjoyed its magic and mystery. Festivals, both religious and non-religious, often take place at night, making use of the darkness to celebrate light – a symbol of goodness and truth in many cultures.

January to February

The new year is welcomed with spectacular festivals all over the world. Chinese New Year arrives with a bang in either January or February, depending on a calendar based on the cycles of the Moon. A little later, the Rio Carnival kicks off in fantastic style.

The leader of the dragon dance entices the dragon with a giant 'pearl' – a balloon or lantern.

Chinese New Year is the most important festival for Chinese families all over the world. It is a time of peace, happiness and success. Houses are cleaned to sweep away any ill-fortune from the previous year, and to welcome in luck for the next.

New Year's Eve begins with a huge feast for all the family – there are even places laid at the table for the spirits of departed ancestors. The menu might include sharks' fins, birds' nests, sea cucumbers and jellyfish. Red lanterns glow all night, and firecrackers are set off at midnight. This is said to scare off Nian, a legendary monster, who is terrified of the colour red, light and loud noises.

Fifteen days later, the celebrations close with the Lantern Festival, during which beautiful lanterns light the streets. Often, there is a dragon dance – a huge dragon made of silk, paper and bamboo weaves through the crowds, led by skilled dancers.

The spectacular Rio Carnival is held every year in Rio de Janeiro in Brazil. A huge parade of floats and samba dancers wearing fantastic feathery costumes weaves its way down the grandest avenue in Rio. The carnival is a Christian Mardi Gras festival, a chance to feast and party before Lent, when some Christians avoid rich food or meat for 40 days. The word 'carnival' comes from the Latin phrase 'carne vale', which means 'goodbye meat'.

March to April

The beginning of spring is celebrated by two very different festivals of fire. In India, Hindus gather around bonfires to celebrate Holi, and at about the same time, the Spanish city of Valencia is lit up for five days during Las Fallas, or 'The Fires'.

Holi begins on the night of the full Moon during the spring harvest. Worshippers gather wood and pile it into huge mounds. Then, priests say prayers before lighting the fires. The flames are thought to point towards land that will be fertile the next year. As the bonfires blaze away, some people sing, beat drums or play horns.

The Holi bonfire is connected to an ancient story about a demoness named Holika and her nephew, the noble prince Prahlad. They both walked into a bonfire, but only Prahlad escaped unharmed.

Offerings of wheat, grain, popcorn, incense and garlands of flowers are placed around the bonfire and later thrown into it. Coconuts, symbols of new life, are roasted in the fire and then eaten as prasuda, or 'holy food'.

Holi is also a festival of colour – a symbol of fertility. People cover each other in brightly coloured powdered paints known as gulal. They mix the powders with water, and squirt them from water pistols and bicycle pumps. Jokes and pranks are played, and everyone has a chance to have fun in the colourful mess.

Cows are sacred in India, so their dung is holy, too. Garlands of cow dung are thrown into some Holi bonfires.

At the beginning of Las Fallas, elaborate statues of historical figures, animals and even popstars are made from wood and plaster, and displayed all over Valencia. Many are as tall as buildings and need to be put into place by cranes. On March 19, St Joseph's feast day, crowds gather for the final night of celebrations. The statues are stuffed with fireworks and the streetlights are turned off. On the stroke of midnight, all the statues – often more than 300 in total – are set alight. Only the crowd's favourite is spared from the flames.

May to June

Tikkun leyl Shavuot is a special night of quiet study for devout Jews, and the candlelit Visakha festival is an important and solemn occasion for Buddhists in Thailand. However, Midsummer's Night in Scandinavia is a lively and loud event with singing and dancing under the midnight Sun.

Tikkun leyl Shavuot is a religious book as well as the name for the night the book is read. At night, heaven is said to receive prayers, so Jews try to pray and read all night. They may have milk and honey, symbols of the Torah – the teachings God delivered to Moses.

Buddha is thought to have been born, enlightened – released from the sufferings of the mind – and to have died on the same day of the year. Visakha honours this day. At dusk, worshippers bring candles, incense and food to monasteries, which they walk around three times as part of the ceremony.

Midsummer's Night in the Northern Hemisphere falls around June 21, when this part of the Earth is tilted directly towards the Sun and receives more sunlight than on any other day. This is the summer solstice – the longest day of the whole year – when night becomes day.

Sweden, Norway, Denmark and Finland are all part of Scandinavia, which sits high in the Northern Hemisphere. They have celebrated Midsummer's Night for thousands of years. The night marks the return of summer and a new season of crops. Many people head to beauty spots among the mountains and lakes. They watch the Sun, which at midnight just touches the horizon, but does not set.

Midsummer's Night is a time of festive fun. Men, women and children dance around maypoles, wearing traditional dress and garlands made from flowers and leaves – symbols of new life. Everyone celebrates by dancing, singing or by feasting on home-made beer and cheese.

Maypoles are often shaped like Christian crosses, as the birth of St John the Baptist is also celebrated on Midsummer's Night.

Accordion players provide music for the maypole dance. Some maypoles have colourful ribbons that are woven around the pole by the dancers.

35

July to August

In the warm nights of July and August, two very special events take place. Sri Lanka's Esala Perahera, with its magnificent procession of elephants, is unmissable, and the colourful Star Festival in Japan remembers two star-crossed lovers.

Every year, on one night in the Buddhist month of Esala – July or August – the streets of Kandy in Sri Lanka are filled with dancers, drummers, acrobats, fire-eaters and, most importantly, elephants. They are all gathered to celebrate the final procession of the spectacular Esala Perahera – a two-week festival held in honour of a single tooth. It is believed that this tooth belonged to Buddha himself.

When Buddha, the 'Enlightened One', died about 2,500 years ago, it is thought that one of his teeth was taken from his funeral pyre and brought to Sri Lanka, hidden in the hair of a princess. Today, the tooth, known as the 'Relic', is kept in a golden casket in the Dalada Maligawa – the Temple of the Tooth.

The lead elephant walks on a carpet of white linen so that it remains pure, its feet never touching the earth.

On the final night of the festival, when the Moon is full, a replica of the Relic is paraded through the streets. It sits proudly under a canopy of electric lights, carried on an elephant known as the Maligawa Tusker. This distinguished elephant is the leader of almost 100 elephants, all decorated in beautiful cloths and bright lights. The city echoes with the sound of drums, cracking whips, the clanging of the elephants' bells and the cheers of the delighted spectators.

The Japanese Star Festival, Tanabata, takes place on July 7. The celebration relates to an ancient Chinese myth about two lovers, Vega and Altair. They were banished to the heavens to become stars separated by the Milky Way. Vega and Altair can reunite only once a year – on July 7 – and on this day, young lovers, some in beautiful traditional dress, meet under the stars. The city of Sendai celebrates Tanabata over three days in August. Love poems and wishes are written on paper streamers and attached to bamboo sticks. These colourful decorations frame the lively street parades.

Talented drummers and dancers perform at the festival. Originally, the Kandyan classical dancing skills were handed down within families from father to son. Today, anyone with talent and dedication can train to become a dancer.

37

September to October

The magical Chinese Moon Festival and Divali, the Hindu festival of lights, both cheer the gloom at this time of year. But Hallowe'en, celebrated all over the world, delights in the darkness and is certainly the spookiest night of the year.

It is traditional to eat tasty mooncakes, made from pastry and delicious fillings, during the Chinese Moon Festival, also known as the Harvest Festival. Families picnic at night, eating the cakes, drinking tea and honouring the Moon, a symbol of abundance and harmony.

Divali, or Deepavali, means 'row of lights'. During this festival, divas, which are tiny clay lamps, are lit after sunset. The lamps welcome home King Rama, who was in exile for 14 years and conquered the demon Ravana. Divali, which celebrates all triumphs of good over evil, is also associated with Lakshmi, the goddess of wealth.

The tradition of Hallowe'en stretches back for many centuries to the ancient Celtic festival of Samhain, meaning 'summer's end'. Samhain took place on October 31, the last night of the Celtic year, and it was a time of witches and warlocks, and of the ghosts of departed souls who were thought to revisit the Earth, seeking revenge.

Hallowe'en takes its name from the Christian adaptation of Samhain – All Hallow's Eve ('hallowed' means 'holy'). However, this night has always been associated with death, evil and the supernatural more than with Christian beliefs. Over time, harmless creatures such as bats, black cats and spiders have developed spooky reputations and are now symbols of Hallowe'en. Mythical beings such as werewolves and vampires are also feared on this night, but today, although people still enjoy old superstitions, Hallowe'en is a festival of fun and not fear.

Trick-or-treating
is a popular Hallowe'en
tradition. Children in fancy
dress visit local homes, asking
for treats of sweets and chocolate
under the playful threat of tricks –
perhaps a few squirts from a water
pistol! In the past, people got
up to all sorts of mischief at
Hallowe'en, taking doors off
hinges, greasing doorknobs
with treacle, and hurling
turnips and cabbages about.
Children should be accompanied
by adults when trick-or-treating.

The carved,
candlelit pumpkin –
the jack-o'lantern – probably
relates to a character called Jack
in Irish folklore. When Jack, who was
very mischievous, died, he wasn't
allowed into heaven. He wasn't
allowed into hell either because he
had tricked even the devil! Instead,
Jack was doomed to walk the Earth
with only a glowing ember in a
hollowed-out turnip to light his
way through the darkness.

November to December

As the year comes to an end, the night-time festivities continue. Important Muslim and Jewish festivals take place, Mexico honours its dead, and England remembers Guy Fawkes with blazing bonfires.

On December 31, at the stroke of midnight, cities all over the world celebrate the start of a new year. In London, England, crowds gather near Big Ben, an historic clock tower, to watch the fireworks.

Eid-ul-Fitr is the huge celebration that marks the end of Ramadan, the ninth and most holy month in the Muslim year. The exact date for this festival varies because the Muslim calendar is lunar – based on the cycles of the Moon. Ramadan is very holy because during this month about 1,400 years ago, the Prophet Muhammad received the first revelation from Allah (God). During Ramadan, Muslims fast from dawn to sunset, only eating or drinking at night. Eid-ul-Fitr, which means the 'Festival of the Breaking of the Fast', begins when the new Moon of the next month, Shawwal, is sighted.

The crescent of the new Moon is a faint sliver and often very difficult to see. People search the night skies with binoculars or small telescopes from high spots around the cities and towns. As soon as they have seen the Moon, they contact religious leaders, or muftis, who organize the official announcement of the end of Ramadan on TV and radio stations.

That night, Muslims all over the world prepare for the festivities of the following day, when families will enjoy a daytime meal for the first time in a month. They clean their houses and lay out their best clothes, ready to receive visitors. They also make gifts and cards to exchange as symbols of blessings and joy. The next morning, just after the Sun has risen, special prayers in the mosques begin the day.

In Mexico, November 1 and 2 are Days of the Dead. People spend whole nights beside their relatives' graves. They decorate the graves with candles to guide souls back to the Earth and with sugar skeletons.

November 5 is Bonfire Night in England. Bonfires are lit to remember Guy Fawkes who tried – and failed – to blow up the English Parliament on this day in 1605. Straw dummies, or 'guys', sit on top of the bonfires.

Hanukkah, the Festival of Lights celebrating the Jewish faith, falls in December. Every night for eight nights, families light a candle on the eight-branched hanukkiyah using a central 'servant' candle.

NIGHT NATURE

When night falls, another world comes
to life in the jungles, deserts, dark skies
and deep oceans. We know about many
of the plants and animals that thrive
in these night-time kingdoms, but some
remain a mystery. You may never see
a shadowy night creature, as most
are shyer than you are, but a rustle,
hoot or howl will tell you it's close by.

Night-time plants

For a few plants, our night is their day. Their sweet-smelling flowers open as the Sun goes down, and they are visited by night-flying insects in search of nectar.

Most flowers open their petals during the day so that they can be pollinated by bees and other daytime insects. When it gets dark, these flowers close their petals to protect their pollen from rain and dew. Insects may get trapped inside the petals, but it's a warm, safe place to spend the night.

The queen of the night cactus, or Moon cactus, is a very unusual plant. It flowers for only one night every year. Some people stay up all night to watch its huge, white petals, which can be 20 centimetres long, unfold. By morning, the fragrant blooms will have died – until the next year.

The flowers of night-blooming plants are usually ghostly white, or the palest yellow or pink – colours that contrast well with the gathering gloom. It is these colours that help moths find the blooms, but as it gets darker, it is the flowers' scents that guide the moths in the right direction. Many flowers such as butterfly orchids and honeysuckles have faint smells during the day, but their night-time perfumes are very strong.

The long, spindly flowers of the honeysuckle make it difficult for most insects to drink the sugary nectar that is inside them. But they are perfectly designed for night-feeding hawk moths, which have long, thin tongues called proboscises that they can insert into the tubes of the flowers.

Flowers that have sour, musty smells attract bats. Hovering like hummingbirds next to the flowers, the bats use their long, wriggly tongues to drink the nectar. Many flowers rely on bats and moths for pollination. The powdery pollen clings onto the night-time visitors and later rubs off onto either the same flower or different flowers, fertilizing them and causing the plants to reproduce.

Night-time animals

As you turn out the light and go to sleep, another world outside your window wakes up and sets off for work. Owls hoot, mice scuttle, bats swoop and slugs slide.

Animals that are awake at night are known as nocturnal. They search for food, find mates and avoid being eaten by predators in almost complete darkness. Fortunately, they have adapted to life with little light and have at least one sense – sight, smell hearing, taste or touch – that is specially good.

Small nocturnal mammals such as hedgehogs have a very good sense of smell, and many animals have large eyes to make the most of every available speck of light.

Some creatures find it easier to hunt at night when there is less competition around. Bats and nightjars scoop up flying insects, which feed swifts and swallows during the day. Owls swoop down onto mice and small birds, which kestrels try to snatch in daylight hours. It is a little bit like shift work!

Creepy-crawlies such as woodlice, centipedes, snails and slugs prefer the dark because it is cool and damp. Their skins are not waterproof, and they lose too much moisture if they come out of their secret hiding places during the day.

Nightjars are very graceful birds. As they fly, they open their bills, or beaks, to try to catch insects.

The red fox is very intelligent. It can adapt to life in woodland, open countryside and even towns.

At dusk, badgers emerge from their setts, or burrows. They feed mostly on fruit, nuts and earthworms.

Snails and slugs leave behind trails of slime as they make their way around damp night-time gardens.

Raccoons are often found in North American towns at night. They search dustbins to find food.

Hedgehogs have thick, prickly coats. When a hedgehog senses danger, it curls up into a tight, spiny ball.

Seeing in the dark

Creatures that come out in the dark of the night usually have much better night vision than humans do. On a black, moonless night, owls, leopards, bushbabies and even pet cats can see shadowy shapes that help them find their way about, hunt for food and hide from danger.

Some animals such as the African bushbaby have a layer of cells called a tapetum at the back of their eyes. The tapetum acts like a mirror, reflecting light. This causes 'eyeshine' – when eyes glow like shiny sequins.

The African leopard, like all members of the cat family, has very good night vision. This powerful hunter preys on baboons and antelopes and any small animals that it can find in the darkness of the bush.

The eyes of nocturnal animals are specially designed to make the most of whatever light is available. They are usually very big with large lenses and extremely sensitive retinas. The retina is the lining at the back of the eye that sends messages to the brain, which interprets what has been seen.

As far as we know, nocturnal animals can see only in black and white, and shades of grey. This is because the light-sensitive cells of their retinas are shaped like rods rather than cones. Rod-shaped cells can detect only whether there is any light or not, whereas it is the cone-shaped cells that detect colour. The retinas of humans contain both 'rods' and 'cones'.

The eyes of some night hunters are so big that they cannot move around in their sockets at all. This means that the creature has to turn its whole head to follow moving objects. Owls, with their huge, saucer-like eyes can swivel their heads right around to stare directly behind themselves.

Pupils are the holes in the centre of eyes' irises, or coloured parts. By day, the pupils of a cat are narrow, vertical slits that stop too much bright light entering the retinas, damaging them.

During the night, a cat's pupils widen and become rounded. This enables as much of the dim light as possible to pass through the pupils to the retinas, helping the cat to see better in the dark.

49

Night Owl

Most owls are efficient and skilful hunters, perfectly designed to swoop silently through the dark night skies. This barn owl, with its distinctive, heart-shaped face, is no exception. The owl's body is small and light, but its wings are huge and powerful, and covered with a velvety down that muffles sound and gives no warning to its victims.

Large, round eyes on flat faces give owls excellent binocular vision in the dimmest of light, but it is their finely tuned sense of hearing that can pick up the tiniest rustle of a dry leaf or the faintest snap of a twig from great distances through the still night air.

The barn owl is sometimes called the 'screech', 'screaming' or 'death' owl because of its strange, unearthly shrieks. Found all over the world, it is a familiar nocturnal owl and is often known simply as the 'night' owl.

When the barn owl detects its prey, it plunges, powerful talons outstretched, and snatches its favourite food – a mouse, rat, frog or bird.

There are about 130 different species of owl found all over the world. The burrowing owl from North and South America lives in abandoned burrows, which it guards during the day. If it is disturbed, it makes buzzing calls to mimic a rattlesnake. During the night, the burrowing owl hunts, and not being keen on flying, it runs along the ground on long, specially adapted legs.

The Australian sooty owl is rarely seen or heard in its dense rainforest habitat. This striking owl is soot coloured with huge, dark eyes, but perhaps is best known for its unusual 'bomb-whistle' call, which sounds like a bomb falling without the final explosion.

The female long-eared owl from Europe, North America and Africa is a fierce defender of her nest. She will distract intruders by pretending to be injured or by flopping about on the ground away from her nest, making strange noises. If this fails, she will spread her wings into a huge fan to appear twice as big – a terrifying sight for any raccoon or hostile owl that crosses her path!

With sharp, hooked beaks, owls tear their prey to pieces and swallow it in chunks. They spit out compact pellets of fur, feathers, bone and anything else they can't digest.

Night bat

At sunset, huge colonies of bats emerge from caves, spiralling in dark clouds high into the sky. The flapping of thousands of pairs of wings sends cool breezes through the night air. A spectacular sight, visible for kilometres, the bats are off to hunt insects and will return just before sunrise.

There are nearly 1,000 species of bat – from Thailand's tiny bumblebee bat to Indonesia's giant flying fox, which has a wingspan of almost two metres. Some bats swoop over lakes and rivers to catch fish, while others drink the nectar from desert cacti. Bats, whose scientific Latin name is 'chiroptera', meaning 'hand-wings', are the only mammals that can truly fly.

Fruit bats, or flying foxes, are large bats with fox-like faces. They live in small groups in trees, and feast on soft fruits.

The world's largest bat colony –
20 to 40 million Mexican free-tailed
bats – lives in the Bracken Cave in
Texas, USA. Every night, they produce
tonnes of guano, or droppings, which
can be used to make fertilizers,
insecticides and medicines.
No wonder witch doctors once
believed bats were magical
and could cure disease!

Bats hang upside
down from the roofs
of caves, safely above
danger. They drop into
the space below them
to swoop into flight.

Vampire bats use
their razor-sharp
teeth to bite cattle.
Their saliva makes
blood flow freely so
they can lap it up.

'Old-man' bats have
very wrinkly faces!
The wrinkles help the
bats make squeaking
noises with their
mouths and noses.

Mexican free-tailed
bats take their name
from their tails, which stick
out beyond the membrane of
their wings. The bats can fly
very fast – up to 100 kilometres per
hour – as they have long, thin wings
and short, velvety fur that reduces
drag, or wind resistance.

The bats hunt moths with the help of echo-location,
which enables them to 'see' in the dark. Every
second, the bats emit between 10 and 20 squeaks –
too high pitched for humans to hear – and then
listen for the returning echoes with their large
ears. Different objects send back different
echoes, and the bats can use this information
to build up a picture of their surroundings.

53

Creepy-Crawlies

You probably share your home
with a few tiny creatures that emerge
when you are fast asleep. These harmless
house guests may leave behind some clues –
a trail of droppings, miniature
footprints or a silken web.

All moths are
attracted to lights.
The beautiful Moon
moth's four wings are
covered in tiny, green scales
that give the moth its striking
colour. The scales rub off easily
and as the moth gets older,
it will become duller in colour.

Woodlice, which
are either sowbugs or
pillbugs, emerge from
their damp hiding places
at night to feed on rotten
wood or decaying plants. Pillbugs
are nicknamed 'roly-polies' because
they can roll up into tight balls,
protecting themselves inside
armour-plated globes.

Crickets are also attracted
to lights and often gather
around them, disturbing
anyone trying to sleep with
a loud, chirping chorus. Only
male crickets make this noise,
rubbing their wings together,
in order to attract females.

Cockroaches are particularly fond of warm
basements, although they can survive freezing
temperatures. Some cockroaches have fully
developed wings that they use to glide
about in the air. Cockroaches are
troublesome creatures that
can spread germs and that
eat anything they can find –
from shoe polish, soap and
ink, to glue and wallpaper!

Before you go
to bed, be careful to clear away
any food left lying around, or
you may be providing a midnight
snack for a hungry mouse! House
mice can give birth to 12 babies at
once more than 10 times a year!

The bedbug is an
unwelcome night visitor.
It can make its home in
mattresses and the cracks and crevices
around beds. It feeds on blood, piercing
the skin of the sleeper with its long beak
and sucking the blood into its stomach.
Bed bugs leave behind a musty smell
rather like raspberries!

The shy house spider,
or cobweb spider, hides in
nooks and crannies during
the day and scurries out at
night to spin its messy web.
It is a helpful night worker,
catching and eating pests
such as flies and mites.

Shiny, speedy silverfish love
damp, dark and cool places,
choosing to live in basements,
kitchens and bathrooms.
They hitchhike into homes
in old books and papers –
their favourite foods!

It is easy to tell when a slug has been
out and about – it leaves behind a silvery,
slimy trail of mucus. This mucus protects
the slug from rough or sharp surfaces –
a slug can crawl along the edge of a razor
blade unharmed. The slime also puts off
predators that do not like gooey meals!

A night in the desert

The porcupine has long, sharp quills that it can thrust into an attacker. The quills remain stuck in the victim, and it can take several months for new quills to grow back.

The tiny African fennec fox has huge ears that act like radiators, giving off excess heat to keep the fox cool. The fox lives in an underground burrow during the day.

The hairy Sun spider is a fierce hunter, devouring lizards, mice and small birds. The spider, which makes its nest with animal hair, bites off the legs of its prey before eating it.

When the scorching desert Sun sets, an army of creatures emerges to look for food. By day, they hide from the heat under rocks or in burrows, but in the cool of the night, they venture out onto the bleak moonlit landscape.

The desert at night can be a hostile place and many animals survive with special skills or weapons. The gila monster is a fearsome lizard with striking yellow-and-black markings that warn its enemies and prey of its poisonous bite. A rattlesnake, buzzing with the rattle at the tip of its tail, can also deliver a venomous bite. Scorpions don't bite, but they do have a poisonous sting at the end of their abdomen.

The coyote, with its mournful howl, is a skilled hunter. As a member of the dog family, it has excellent senses of smell and hearing, and can run very fast.

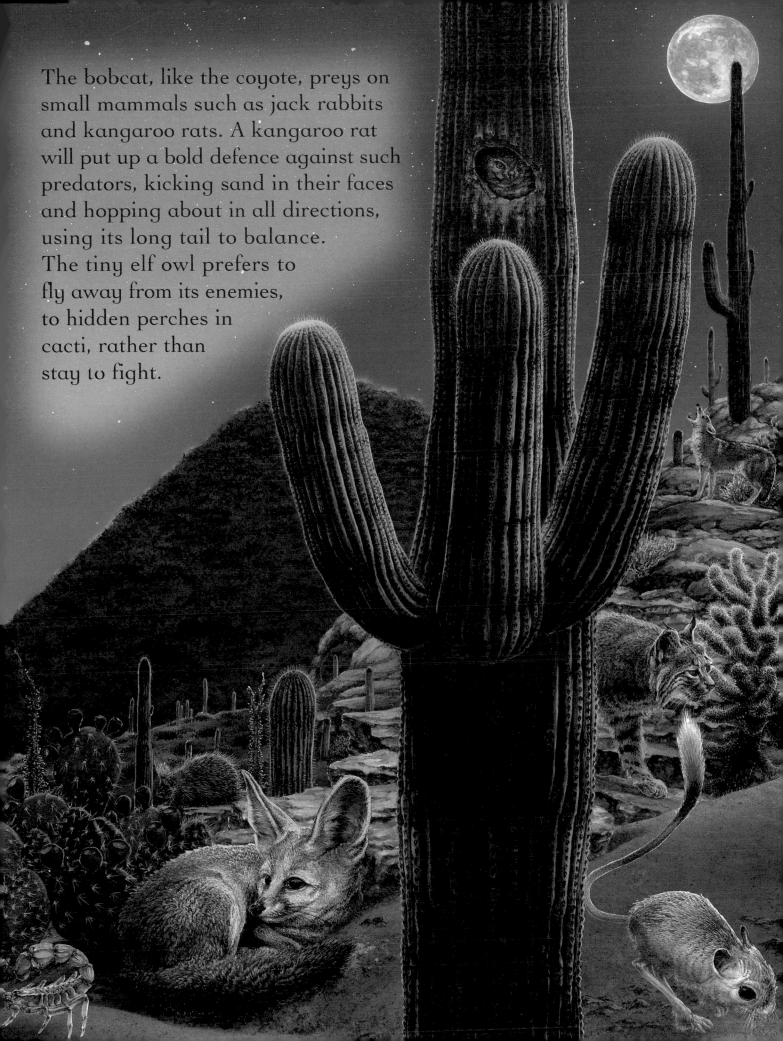

The bobcat, like the coyote, preys on
small mammals such as jack rabbits
and kangaroo rats. A kangaroo rat
will put up a bold defence against such
predators, kicking sand in their faces
and hopping about in all directions,
using its long tail to balance.
The tiny elf owl prefers to
fly away from its enemies,
to hidden perches in
cacti, rather than
stay to fight.

A night at Sea

When the Sun's rays have dimmed and the oceans turn an inky black, different sea creatures glow and shine in the darkness. 'Sea fire' sparkles on the surface of tropical waters, and in the depths, squid glow, while flashlight fish rotate their lights to search for food, safe from daytime predators.

Sea fire, or phosphorescence, carpets the sea in a glittering, orange light. It is produced by thousands of tiny sea organisms called plankton. The plankton glow when they are moved about in the waves — perhaps by schools of dolphins using echo-location to hunt for fish in the dark.

For the creatures that inhabit the deepest ocean depths, there is no difference between night and day — they live in permanent darkness. Many deep-sea fish are blind and feel their way around with tiny sensors. Others have special taste buds that tell them about their surroundings. Some fish have eyes that face upwards to peer at the dim silhouettes and shadows nearer the surface.

The transparent bell and short tentacles of the Moon jellyfish seem to glow a milky white in the dark. The jellyfish expands and contracts its bell to push water out to propel itself along.

The wobbegong shark, or carpet shark, hunts for fish in the night. During the day, it lies on the ocean floor and uses the fringes around its mouth to disguise itself as seaweed.

The seahorse is a very unusual marine animal – the male seahorse gives birth! He will anchor hImself to coral with his curly tail so that the female seahorse can lay her eggs in his pouch.

The bat starfish, like many starfish, can tell night from day by using the light-sensitive tips on the end of each arm. Some starfish are drawn to the light, while others prefer to stay in the dark.

Some angler fish disguise themselves as seaweed and lure fish into their mouths with fins that look like worms. Deep-sea angler fish have lights on the end of these 'fishing rods' to attract fish.

Cuttlefish put on one of the best underwater light shows. If they are agitated, electric blue spots and flashes of light pulse along their bodies. The colours are made by small sacks in their skin.

Nature glows

The night-time darkness of dense, tropical rainforests is lit by bioluminescence — light that is produced naturally by all kinds of different plants and insects.

Fireflies are nocturnal winged beetles that use light signals to attract mates. The orange or green glows from their abdomens are produced by chemical reactions.

The rare railway worm from South America is a firefly larva. It has a red glowing 'headlamp' and rows of luminous green spots along its body that look like railway signals.

The cucujo beetle is the most luminous insect of all. Long ago, they were used instead of candles, and people tied them to their feet to light their way. Girls even wore them as hair decorations!

Fireflies, found all over the world, are a common cause of natural, night-time glows. Their luminous, worm-like offspring, or larvae, are known as glow-worms, as are some female wingless fireflies. They gather in trees in their thousands, continuously flashing their lights in time with each other, sometimes for months on end.

The yellow jack-o'lantern mushroom produces a greenish glow from the gills on its underside. Like many fungi, it is poisonous.

Mushrooms known as 'fox fire' glow blue, yellow and green on damp forest floors. The white petals of the Moon flower seem to glow in the moonlight.

One centipede from Asia produces luminous secretions from in between its segments, giving it a stripy glow. Mammals or amphibians are not bioluminescent — but some frogs eat so many fireflies that they glow from the inside!

NIGHT WORKERS

Many people traditionally work at night – bakers produce fresh bread for the morning, and fishing crews bring their catch into shore before sunrise. Astronomers stargaze in the darkness, and doctors and nurses are ready at any time of night to treat the sick. Some tasks are easier when less people are up and about – spare a thought for the workers that clean, repair and maintain our railways, roads, shops and offices while we are tucked up in bed.

Night flight

Long ago, when travellers used to rely on the stars and the Moon to guide them on their way, journeys by night could often be a risky business. Today, skilled pilots, flight attendants and air-traffic controllers, using sophisticated equipment, ensure that passengers are transported safely all around the world on long flights through the night skies.

Air-traffic controllers use radar to monitor aircraft. They give pilots permission to take off and land, and ensure that the aeroplanes keep safe distances from each other.

At night, aircraft marshals use illuminated wands to guide aircraft around the airport. Some airports, particularly those in built-up areas, restrict the number of aeroplanes that are allowed to take off and land during the night

As passengers on night flights are fast asleep, tucked under blankets, huge jet engines carry them through the darkness at speeds of up to 900 kilometres per hour. In the cockpit, the pilot and co-pilot are wide awake in front of hundreds of dials and instruments, switches and levers that wink and shine in the darkness. The equipment shows exactly where the aircraft is, how fast it is going, how high it is flying and how well the engines are running. From the nose of the aeroplane, radars scan the gloom for other aircraft or for brewing storms. Screens in the cockpit display all the findings from the radars.

The on-board computer can take over to give the pilots a well-deserved break. In between take-off and landing, the aeroplane can fly safely on autopilot for many thousands of kilometres.

During long night flights, the team of attendants pull down the blinds and dim the main lights so that the passengers can relax and go to sleep. They also supply headphones so that people can listen to music or watch films on TV screens. Passengers can read under individual overhead lights. The flight attendants serve ready-made breakfasts, lunches and dinners.

It is very important to be as comfortable as possible on long-distance night flights – and to get some sleep if you can! Airlines often supply passengers with bedtime packs that may include a comb, a toothbrush and toothpaste, an eye mask, socks or slippers, and a blanket.

Night nursing

Hospitals are staffed night and day,
365 days a year, ready to nurse the sick.
Highly skilled doctors and nurses work hard,
handling emergencies and performing surgery,
as well as delivering babies, who make their
entrance no matter what time of night it is!

Hospitals don't stop during the night – they must keep ticking over like well-oiled machines. Teams of doctors, nurses, cleaners, receptionists and porters keep things running smoothly and handle the people that stream into the hospital at all hours. The night shift begins when the day teams go home.

Most operations are scheduled to take place during the day. However, some operations are extremely complicated and can last more than ten hours, often continuing into the night. Surgeons, nurses and anaesthetists work together to carry out the surgery. Operating theatres are available at night to deal with emergencies.

In the accident and emergency department, 'A & E' or 'casualty', the hospital staff need to be ready for any patients that the paramedics might bring to them in ambulances. The paramedics perform on-the-spot medical care at the scenes of accidents, but they must hurry to transport the sick and injured to the hospital, where doctors can provide more extensive care with better equipment. The paramedics often radio the hospital as they speed through the night in the ambulances, so that the staff can make preparations for their arrival. The staff in A & E are always very busy, finding beds for everyone, referring patients to surgeons and working hard to save lives.

The hospital wards
are quieter during the night.
The out-patients, who do not stay the night, and all the visitors
have left long ago. The in-patients, asleep in their beds, are
watched over by night nurses. Specially trained nurses monitor
patients recovering from surgery in intensive care units. Every
night, many doctors are 'on call' – they can be called into action
at any time of the night to deal with emergencies or to check
patients in the wards. In between, they try to snatch a little sleep
in small hospital bedrooms, or have a cup of tea and a rest.

The baker

Bakers work through the night so that fresh bread is ready for us each morning. Today, most bread is baked in huge factories, but there are still some small bakeries that bake and sell delicious breads, cakes and biscuits.

Baking bread can be a tricky, lengthy task, and traditional bakers are very skilled. Early in the morning, long before the Sun rises, bakers begin work in the small kitchens behind bakery shops.

Pressing and squeezing with their hands, they knead the dough – a mixture of flour, water and yeast – and leave it to prove, or rise. They cut and roll it into shape – sometimes creating complex swirls or plaits. Then, the dough is baked, often in wood-fired ovens. The bakers may also prepare cakes and buns, which they display with the bread, fresh from the oven, in the shop windows.

Huge, modern bakeries are equipped with all the latest machines that carry out every stage of the bread-making process. Giant industrial mixers whirr and hum, preparing the dough, and stainless steel 'travelling' ovens roar like hungry furnaces, baking the thousands of identical loaves that pass through them on conveyor belts. Different machines then cool, slice and wrap the loaves. The bread is loaded onto lorries and delivered to shops, ready for the morning. These factories work around the clock, seven days a week, and the night shift is the busiest time – 12,000 loaves can be produced in an hour. A team of people operates the machinery and makes sure everything runs smoothly.

Different types of bread

A baguette is a long, thin French loaf of bread. It is often known as a 'French stick' and it is white and fluffy beneath its golden crust.

The dough of pitta bread does not fully rise as it contains too little yeast. Mexican tortillas are 'unleavened' flat breads – they contain no yeast at all.

Pumpernickel is a dark, slightly sour German bread. It is made with coarse rye flour and is usually baked in long, square loaves.

Nightly news

Today, we expect to be able to find out what's going on in the world at any time of day or night. A huge number of people work all night long, gathering and reporting news for television, radio, the internet and newspapers.

There is no such thing as day or night at a live TV news channel – just one long, rolling broadcast that carries on around the clock. Satellites beam live news and pictures all over the world, so that millions of viewers can watch 24 hours a day.

TV news presenters must be alert even if it is the middle of the night. They are helped by autocues – electronic devices near the camera that display scripts. The presenters must always be prepared for the unexpected – a big story suddenly breaking, a technical problem or a guest who doesn't answer the questions!

70

The presenter and the rest of the studio team must listen carefully to the director, who gives instructions from the gallery during the programme, using a system called 'talkback'.

Working hard behind the scenes, a team of researchers gathers information from special agencies and services to prepare news bulletins.

Reporters in 'hot spots' all around the world keep in constant touch with newsrooms and deliver stories to them by satellite links.

The gallery looks like the cockpit of a spaceship, full of switches and dials, buttons and lights. From here, the director monitors the studio on a bank of screens that shows different camera angles. He or she can also view video recordings that need to be woven into programmes, and organize live interviews.

Journalists write at night to get the latest news into the next day's newspaper. Only a few people operate printing presses, which print thousands of copies at a time.

71

Night fishing

The men and women who work on board night fishing boats do not have an easy job. In the darkness, as they haul up their heavy nets of fish, they battle against rough seas, stormy weather and sometimes even sharks!

Fishing crews often need to travel far from land to find fish in the deep oceans, and their trips can last for several days. The crews trawl for fish all through the night to make the most of their time at sea. Every few hours, they haul their nets out of the water, hoping for large catches. They empty the fish onto the decks and then lower the nets back into the dark seas.

In between every haul of fish, the crew must try to get some food and sleep – no easy task if the boat is rolling from side to side on crashing waves! While some of the crew rest, the skipper must keep control of the boat from the wheelhouse.

Larger boats use sonar and computer systems to find big schools of fish. The crews of smaller boats, however, use more traditional methods. An experienced skipper can spot large schools shining in the moonlight near the surface of the water. Hungry seagulls or dolphins in search of fish suppers also guide the way – but the boats must hurry before the fish are eaten! If the crews are really lucky, the lights on their fishing boats will attract fish to them.

Once the fish have been caught, the crews pack them in ice to keep them fresh. Sometimes smaller boats deliver their catches to large factory ships that clean, gut, package and freeze the fish, ready for delivery to shops.

Nets are not the only devices for catching fish. Explosives blast fish out of the water, and electric shocks stun them. In Asia, some people train otters to do their fishing for them!

The three main types of net used in the fishing industry

Purse seines circle fish and then are pulled shut by lines that act like purse strings. They catch pelagic, or surface, fish such as tuna, salmon and anchovy.

Trawl nets, or trawls, are funnel-shaped nets that are dragged along the sea bed to catch demersal, or deep-sea, fish such as cod, sole and haddock.

Gill nets trap fish by their gills. Some gill nets used to drift along and catch every type of sea life. These drift nets, known as 'walls of death', are now banned.

The astronomer

Throughout history, people have gazed up into space in awe. The Ancient Greeks were the first astronomers to list all the stars they could see with the naked eye. Today, professional astronomers use powerful telescopes and modern technology to discover what is really out there.

Telescopes work best at night because there is less light pollution from the Sun, and objects in space stand out clearly against the dark sky. Astronomers often work late into the night to get the best views of space.

Astronomers are skilled scientists, technicians and engineers who work together to collect and analyze electronic information from telescopes. Telescopes act as giant cameras that take pictures of space, but it is possible to look through them directly. Professional astronomers from all over the world travel to large observatories to spend a few precious nights observing stars and galaxies that are millions of light years away.

Telescopes are housed in observatories, which are usually built in remote places, far from the light pollution caused by the bright lights from cities. The best locations are deserts, where the night skies are clear and cloudless, or mountain tops, above the clouds and city smog.

Mauna Kea, a dormant volcano in Hawaii, is home to many observatories that dot the barren landscape with their space-age domes. The domes, eight storeys high, protect their telescopes from wind and rain. All day, air conditioners keep the temperature inside the domes near freezing so that when the roofs open at night, the telescopes aren't affected by the cold night air.

NIGHT SKY

When you look up at the sky on a clear,
cloudless night, thousands of stars shine
and twinkle in the velvety darkness.
Their light has travelled billions of
kilometres through space. Much nearer,
you'll see the Moon, our closest neighbour,
and you may even see a planet, shining
steadily. They are all part of our galaxy,
the Milky Way, which, even without
a telescope, can be a spectacular sight.

Night and day

We know that darkness falls and temperatures drop during the night, but why does this happen? To find the answer, we must look at the bigger picture out in space, and discover how night is caused by the movements of our planet, the Earth, and its star, the Sun. Occasionally, the Moon also plays a part, turning day into night as it eclipses the Sun.

As the Earth orbits the Sun in huge loops, it spins on its axis, an imaginary line running through its centre from the North Pole to the South Pole. It takes 24 hours to complete its spin. As the Earth revolves, the part of it that faces the Sun, receiving its light and warmth, experiences day. The rest of the planet is plunged into the darkness of night. When it is day in Africa, on the other side of the globe in North and South America, it is night.

Day becomes night during an eclipse of the Sun, or solar eclipse. When the Moon, which orbits the Earth, moves in between the Earth and the Sun, it casts a shadow onto the Earth. The small area that lies directly in the Moon's shadow experiences a total eclipse. A larger, partly shadowed area experiences a partial eclipse. The Sun is about 400 times larger than the Moon, but the Moon is about 400 times closer to the Earth. This means that when we observe a total eclipse, the Moon appears to completely cover the Sun.

The length of night and day varies because the Earth's axis tilts and as it completes its orbit of the Sun, different parts of the planet are tipped towards the Sun at different times of the year. From May to August, the Northern Hemisphere is tipped towards the Sun, so it experiences summer. This means that as the Earth spins around, light from the Sun hits the Northern Hemisphere for longer each day during its summer, causing longer days and shorter nights. During the same months, the Southern Hemisphere, tilted away from the Sun and receiving less sunlight, experiences winter, with short days and long nights. Areas near the equator are angled towards the Sun at all times of year. This means that they don't have any seasons, and the days and nights are always about the same length.

The Moon

The Moon is the biggest and brightest object in our night sky. Although it seems to glow, it has no light of it own, but reflects light from the Sun. It appears so large only because it is close to us in space. In fact, it is much smaller than all the stars, which look tiny.

It is not difficult to understand why the Moon, with its beautiful pale light, was worshipped in ancient times. In Greece, the Moon was represented by the goddess Selene, who drove a two-horse chariot across the night skies. In Ancient Egypt, the Moon god Thoth was worshipped. He had a human body and the head of an ibis – a wading bird.

During its cycles, the Moon waxes and wanes, or grows and shrinks, changing from a tiny, silver sliver into a large, shining globe, and back again. Long ago, some people believed that a full Moon could cause madness. The word 'lunatic', meaning 'insane' or 'mad', comes from the Latin word 'luna', which means 'Moon'.

The Moon appears to change shape as different parts of it reflect the Sun's light during its orbit around the Earth. The different shapes are known as the phases of the Moon.

NEW MOON

WAXING CRESCENT

FIRST QUARTER

WAXING GIBBOUS

Different types of craters on the Moon's surface

A terraced crater has sides like huge, steep steps, and mountains in its centre.

A concentric crater looks like a series of smaller rings inside larger rings.

A ray crater has streaks, or rays, of light-coloured rocks surrounding it.

A ghost crater is an old crater, almost totally filled in by molten rock.

A 'moon' is a rocky object that orbits a planet. Our Moon is about four billion years old. As it orbits the Earth, it spins on its axis, keeping the same side facing towards the Earth. On this side, we can see both light and dark patches. The light patches are mountains, valleys and craters. The craters, some more than 200 kilometres wide, were formed by asteroids crashing onto the Moon's surface. The dark patches are vast plains created by molten rock that cooled and hardened millions of years ago. They are known as 'maria', the Latin for 'seas', but they don't contain water. The Sea of Tranquillity and the Ocean of Storms are maria on the Moon.

FULL MOON

WANING GIBBOUS

LAST QUARTER

WANING CRESCENT

OLD MOON

81

Eclipse of the Moon

**Every so often, we are treated to a
very special night-time performance
when the Moon darkens and turns
a magnificent, coppery red colour.
This strange sight is caused
by an eclipse of the Moon.**

When the Earth eclipses,
or casts its shadow over,
the Moon, it is known as an
eclipse of the Moon, or a lunar
eclipse. This occurs when the
Moon is on the opposite side
of the Earth to the Sun. As the
Earth lies directly between
the Sun and the Moon, it blocks
light reaching the Moon and
casts its dark shadow over it.

The Moon normally glows brightly
because it reflects light from the Sun.
When the Moon is eclipsed, it receives
no light directly from the Sun, so it
appears darker. The Moon does not
completely disappear from sight during a
lunar eclipse, but it glows an orangey red. This
is because a small amount of light from the Sun is
able to filter through the Earth's atmosphere into the
Earth's shadow and bathe the Moon in a coppery glow.

Throughout history, people have watched eclipses, lunar and solar, in both fear and fascination, amazed by unusual events that many believed were the work of gods.

In 1504, Christopher Columbus, the famous Italian explorer, took advantage of such beliefs. When he was marooned on the island of Jamaica, the local people refused to give him food. Columbus knew that a lunar eclipse was predicted for February 29, so he arranged a meeting with the people on that night. Columbus told them that God was so angry with them that he was going to take the Moon away. When the eclipse happened right on cue, the people were so frightened that they gave food to Columbus immediately!

No special equipment is needed to observe lunar eclipses – there is no bright sunlight to damage your eyes – but a pair of binoculars or a small telescope will help you get a closer look. Then, all you need to do is hope for clear skies and enjoy the show.

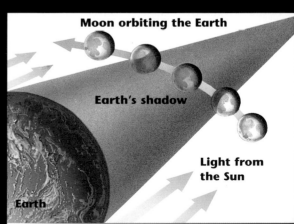

Moon orbiting the Earth

Earth's shadow

Light from the Sun

Earth

When all of the Moon is completely covered by the Earth's shadow, people on the part of the Earth that faces the Moon will see a total lunar eclipse. When the Moon is only partly shadowed during its orbit, a partial lunar eclipse will be seen. The Moon orbits the Earth about every 27 days, but lunar eclipses occur only up to three times a year. This is because the Moon does not pass through the Earth's shadow every time it orbits the Earth.

Men On the Moon

Over the years, there have been many weird and wonderful stories about the Moon. An early science-fiction story described a Moon that was inhabited by fleas twelve times the size of elephants! Today, we no longer have to invent stories about the Moon – on July 20, 1969, two men actually walked on its surface.

American astronauts Neil Armstrong and Edwin 'Buzz' Aldrin touched down on the Moon's surface in their lunar module, the Eagle, as part of NASA's Apollo 11 mission in 1969. Armstrong famously declared, "The Eagle has landed."

As commander of the mission, Armstrong was the first to step out of the Eagle, and in doing so, he made history, becoming the first human to set foot on the Moon. Followed closely by Aldrin, Armstrong set up a TV camera so that the world could watch live their first weightless steps. The two astronauts left behind a plaque.

> **Here men from the planet Earth first set foot upon the Moon, July 1969. We came in peace for all mankind.**

Armstrong and Aldrin carried out experiments, collecting soil samples and taking photographs. Since their historic landing, there have been five more Apollo missions to the Moon. We now know that the Moon is a dry, dead world with no air, wind or weather, and definitely no giant fleas!

Nine planets, including the Earth, orbit the Sun as part of our solar system. The six planets closest to the Earth – Mercury, Venus, Mars, Jupiter, Saturn and Uranus – are just visible to the naked eye in some parts of the Earth's night sky.

MERCURY is hard to see from the Earth as it is so close to the Sun's glare. It orbits the Sun faster than all the other planets, taking just 88 days.

VENUS is the hottest planet – up to 480°C – as its thick atmosphere traps the Sun's heat.

THE EARTH looks blue from space as two thirds of its surface is covered by ocean. Formed about 4.6 billion years ago, its atmosphere contains a lot of oxygen, which makes life possible.

MARS is known as the Red Planet because iron-rich dust has turned its surface and sky red. Scientists believe that life in the form of bacteria could exist on Mars because space probes that have landed on the planet discovered that water once existed there.

THE SUN, a huge ball of hot gas, is our nearest star, and it is so large that more than one million planet Earths would fit inside it. Its size creates a large gravitational pull that keeps the nine planets spinning around it in orbit.

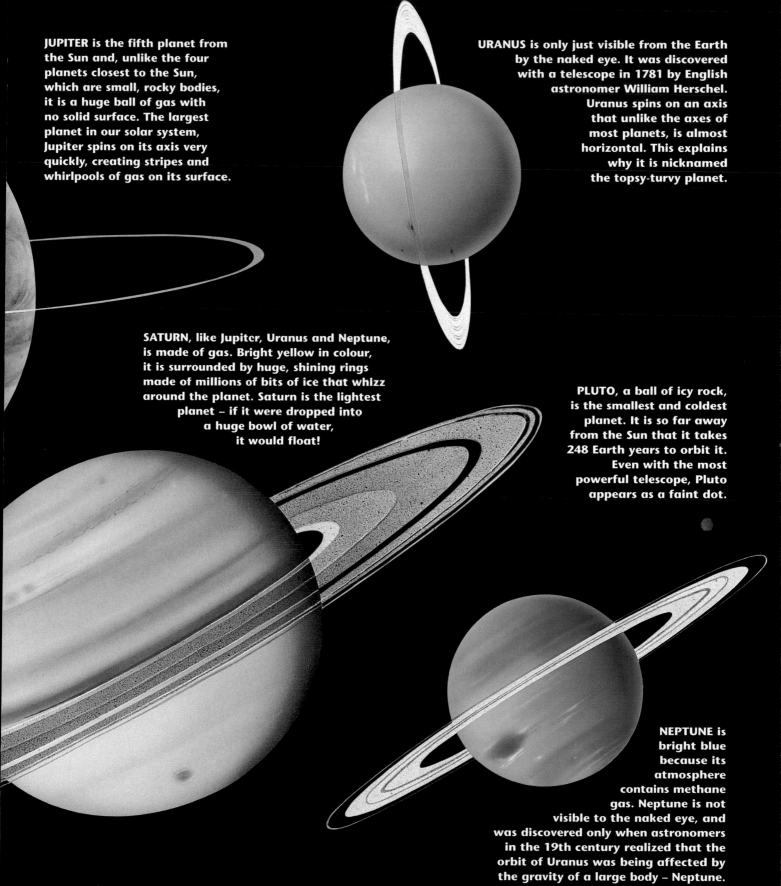

JUPITER is the fifth planet from the Sun and, unlike the four planets closest to the Sun, which are small, rocky bodies, it is a huge ball of gas with no solid surface. The largest planet in our solar system, Jupiter spins on its axis very quickly, creating stripes and whirlpools of gas on its surface.

URANUS is only just visible from the Earth by the naked eye. It was discovered with a telescope in 1781 by English astronomer William Herschel. Uranus spins on an axis that unlike the axes of most planets, is almost horizontal. This explains why it is nicknamed the topsy-turvy planet.

SATURN, like Jupiter, Uranus and Neptune, is made of gas. Bright yellow in colour, it is surrounded by huge, shining rings made of millions of bits of ice that whizz around the planet. Saturn is the lightest planet – if it were dropped into a huge bowl of water, it would float!

PLUTO, a ball of icy rock, is the smallest and coldest planet. It is so far away from the Sun that it takes 248 Earth years to orbit it. Even with the most powerful telescope, Pluto appears as a faint dot.

NEPTUNE is bright blue because its atmosphere contains methane gas. Neptune is not visible to the naked eye, and was discovered only when astronomers in the 19th century realized that the orbit of Uranus was being affected by the gravity of a large body – Neptune.

The Universe

The Moon, stars and planets are all part of our galaxy, the Milky Way, a huge spiralling collection of glittering stars. With the aid of powerful telescopes, we can look at beautiful and amazing things in other parts of the Universe.

Galaxy NGC 4603 is a spiral galaxy like the Milky Way. The 'arms' of this galaxy are made of young, bright-blue stars and red giant stars. A red giant is a huge red star that has expanded greatly and is near the end of its life.

Andromeda, another spiral galaxy, is the nearest major galaxy to us in the Universe. It is 2.2 million light years away, but amazingly it is visible in our night sky. It is the most distant object that we can see without a telescope.

A supernova is a huge star that collapses and then is torn apart in an explosion brighter than billions of our Suns put together. On telescope images, a supernova appears as a small but bright flash of colour, surrounded by rings of debris.

The Universe is everything that exists anywhere – all solid, liquid and gaseous matter. It is too vast to imagine, and when we study the night sky, even with powerful telescopes, we can see only a tiny fraction of it. The Universe contains billions of galaxies, which themselves contain billions of stars, gas and dust particles that collect together because of their gravitational pull.

Our galaxy, the Milky Way, is a spiral galaxy – it has a central bulge with several arms spiralling around it. The Sun, our nearest star, lies in an arm of the Milky Way called the Orion Arm. Distances in the Universe are so vast that we measure them in light years. The Milky Way is about 100,000 light years across – light takes about 100,000 years to travel across the galaxy.

A nebula is a vast cloud of dust and gas. Many nebulae are 'nurseries' where new stars are born. At the heart of some nebulae, fiercely hot stars heat the gas, making it glow beautifully like a huge cavern lit by colourful lanterns.

Butterfly nebulae are also known as 'twin-jet' nebulae. If the nebula is sliced in half, it looks like the two exhausts of a jet engine. The nebula's gas travels at more than 300 kilometres per second – like a very powerful jet engine.

Some of the stars that we see shining like pinpoints in our night sky are about 1,000 light years away. When we see these stars, we are seeing light that has taken 1,000 years to reach us, so we are seeing the stars as they looked 1,000 years ago. By the time their light reaches us, the stars that we see may have changed, exploded or even disappeared without us ever knowing.

International Space Station, or ISS, orbits the Earth. It will be finished in 2004. Huge solar panels, or arrays, absorb heat from the Sun and power the station. The arrays reflect the Sun's light, making ISS visible to the naked eye at night.

Natural fireworks

A comet streaking through the inky night sky, its tail trailing behind it for millions of kilometres, is one of the most spectacular sights to be seen from the Earth.

Thousands of years ago, a comet would have filled the hearts of our ancestors with fear and dread. They believed that comets were omens of doom that caused death, disaster, wars and plagues. Today, we know that comets are lumps of ice and rock travelling in huge, looping orbits around the Sun. There are a vast number of comets in the outer regions of our solar system.

Meteors, or shooting stars, the tiny grains of dust left behind by comets as they swoop past the Sun, can be seen burning up in the atmosphere on most nights of the year. But at certain times, there are meteor showers when you can see as many as 60 meteors in a single hour. This happens when the Earth travels through huge clouds of comet debris, and the meteor showers light up the skies like natural firework displays. Watch out for the Perseids around August 12, and the Geminids just before the middle of December.

A comet's tail can be millions of kilometres in length.

The beautiful Northern and Southern Lights – the Aurora Borealis and the Aurora Australis – are dazzling, natural light shows. They take place around the North and South Poles respectively, and occur when electrically charged particles from the Sun are drawn into the Earth's magnetic field. The glowing curtain of red-and-green light that we see is the result of these particles slamming into the uppermost fringes of our atmosphere.

A comet's orbit leads it on a regular flying visit close to the Sun from the furthest reaches of our solar system. As it gets nearer to the Sun, it starts to evaporate in the heat, and grows a gigantic tail of gas and dust.

Halley's Comet, last visible from the Earth between 1985 and 1986, is named after the English scientist Edmond Halley. He was the first to suggest that comets orbit the Sun. He spotted this particular comet in 1682, and calculated that it would pass by the Earth every 76 years. Comet Hale-Bopp was one of the brightest comets of the last century. It was visible to the naked eye for 19 months during 1996 and 1997.

1. PEGASUS

Pegasus is an immortal winged horse. It is one of 48 constellations named in AD150 by the Greek astronomer Ptolemy.

2. HERCULES

Hercules is another figure from Greek mythology. He was famous for his immense strength and, some say, size.

3. URSA MAJOR

Ursa Major, the Great Bear, is not too hard to see. The seven stars in its tail and lower back are known as the Plough constellation.

4. LEO

Leo, the Lion, is one of the twelve signs of the Zodiac. It is one of the few patterns that resembles what it is supposed to be!

Look to the stars

For thousands of years, people have looked up to the stars and tried to make sense of them. Ancient astronomers imagined that the patterns of shining stars were gods and goddesses, birds, animals and fish. These star patterns belong to sections of the sky we now call constellations.

Constellations over the Northern Hemisphere

When we look up into the night sky, we can imagine a never-ending dome of stars that surrounds us. This is known as the Celestial Sphere. The sphere is divided into a northern and a southern hemisphere – just like the Earth. The stars in each hemisphere can be mapped onto two flat circles.

More than 3,000 years ago, astronomers in the city of Babylonia made rough maps of the patterns that the brightest stars made. They also observed the Sun, the Moon and planets as they moved across a narrow band of stars. They came to the conclusion that this band of stars had an important effect on the lives of people on the Earth and they divided the band into 12 constellations. Each constellation of stars represented a sign of the Zodiac. Today, astrologers use the Zodiac to try to predict the future.

Constellations over the Southern Hemisphere

The Celestial Sphere is divided into 88 sections known as constellations. Each constellation contains a pattern of glittering stars that astronomers have named over the years. Constellations in the southern celestial sphere can only be seen from the Earth's Southern Hemisphere – the Southern Cross cannot be seen in the Northern Hemisphere.

Constellations in the Southern Hemisphere's sky

5. PHOENIX

The Phoenix is the firebird from ancient Arabian mythology. Every 500 years, it set fire to itself and rose again from the ashes.

6. SCORPIO

Scorpio, the Scorpion, is another sign of the Zodiac. Its brightest star, Antares, is 10,000 times more luminous than our star the Sun.

7. LIBRA

Libra, known as the Scales or the Balance, is a small and quite faint constellation. It is the seventh sign of the Zodiac.

8. CRUX

Crux, the Southern Cross, is the smallest constellation of both hemispheres. Crux is a Latin word that means 'cross'.

NEW DAWN

As dawn breaks, the Sun creeps up and slowly steals the scene from night with its pale and brilliant glow. The vast, mysterious expanse of darkest night retreats and vanishes – until next time…

INDEX